Ransomed by Love

The Gift of Jesus

Mary Elizabeth OCDS

Executive Press Ltd
Edmonton AB T6A 0H7
Canada
343-554-1210

Paperback ISBN: 979-8-9987482-7-1
Ebook ISBN: 979-8-9987482-8-8

Dedication

To Joy
Who loves and prays for us all
A wonderful friend
And
A wonderful Carmelite

RANSOMED BY LOVE
The gift of Jesus
Mary Elizabeth OCDS

In this book of reflections and poems I share my astonishment at the communication between my soul and Jesus, my loving Saviour.

My spiritual path has been arduous-common to many- but which journey has brought many blessings. I have indeed been ransomed by Love.

Love with a capital 'L' means the special and unique Love of God for each soul.

I have had to learn to listen to God in my heart, meaning the spiritual centre of who we are. And there discover my soul where within the soul's depth the Spirit of God dwells. The place of loving meeting where God teaches and guides us, always for good. A place of stillness, deep quietness.

I have had to learn to become still. God is very patient! He waits for us to grow.

INTRODUCTION

I will take you through a mixture of poems, they speak of Jesus, Our Saviour and Lord. Mary, the Mother of God, and how the soul travels on the journey of faith, self discovery and peace.

I hope that you will find them refreshing and encouraging.

Mary Elizabeth OCDS

Come, rise in my heart
And let your peace
Bring joy and hope
Never to fade away
Despite life's struggles.

I am weak but You are strong
Always loving
Patient and merciful
Still- in the silence
Deep down in my heart
Waiting for me to come
And rest.

The peace of rest
Like streams of living water
Restoring my soul
The heat of my mind
Bathed, cooled and stilled.
Such gentle Love.

20/4/25

1

When I lift up to You this prayer
I enter the stream of forgiveness
That flows from Your heart
Like a mantle over all creation.
It is so beautiful.
All sin and heartbreak is held in LOVE
But awaits our plea
To enter the stream of healing
A kaleidoscope of moments,
Hours, days, months , maybe even years
Of gentle and tender care ,
Seeping into the soul and spirit
To comfort and strengthen.

Our faithful and loving Lord.

23/4/2025

I desire to live in this stillness

Where I can hear nothing but silence

This tender, gentle presence

That covers my whole being

A mantle of grace

Like a mist reminiscent of dew

Forming coolness on my tired spirit

Giving complete and utter rest.

4/8/24

I am held in gentleness
Like a warm sea
Where there is no end.
So peaceful in my exhaustion.
So many battles fought,
So many wounds
But scars of Love's overcoming
Where the spear's thrust
Attempted death and failed.

I was held all these years
In your wounds, ignorant of Your care
Until You revealed the beauty of Your triumph
And I cried with relief.
Though weak I was strengthened.
I sat on a rock on the shore,
Dazed, gazed at this little pool beside me
And saw in the reflection
Your Sacred Heart holding mine
For all Eternity.

Palm Sunday

24/3/24.

Many years ago I had this' vision' or I saw in my mind's eye, maybe even in my heart, the place of all encounter, the body of the dead Jesus in the tomb; it became surrounded by fiery red spiritual energy and His human body was absorbed or subsumed into it and it became His resurrection body. As a result He could appear to Mary in recognisable form, He could go through locked doors to be with His disciples. He could also walk with 2 disciples on the road to Emmaus in the disguise of a stranger until He revealed Himself in the breaking of bread at supper and then vanished.

I am so grateful to have been shown this. He indeed rose from the dead, body and soul into this new form. And He has appeared, since these early days of the Church, many times through the centuries to bless, encourage and also warn humanity to follow the path of Truth and Love.

You are so close

O Trinity of Love

Not even a breath away.

Your Spirit surrounds me

In a union of separates

My humanity and your Divinity

But a Divinity that has embraced humanity

And healed its' pain,

The Divinity that indwells me

But in depths I have to explore

For there Your Beauty

Will transfigure my spirit

And we will be one

26-27/4/2022

I saw Your Beauty, hidden

But veiled

Patiently waiting

To reveal Yourself in

Your Eternal sacrifice

Through mystical transformation of the bread and wine

And Love the souls You gave Your life for.

You lived the world's horror

Transmuted the pain

And brought Peace

Into the gentle Host

And renewing wine.

Our Jesus, Saviour of all.

26/1/2024 Before the Tabernacle

Joy, like bells ringing in my heart,

Jesus is risen! He waits for each soul

To come to Him. He calls so gently,

This loving shepherd, listening patiently

For our cry of recognition.

He knows each sheep,

All individual characteristics, weaknesses and strengths,

Caring so tenderly, lovingly protecting and guiding us

Over the rough ground of this world

To His wonderful pastures of peace.

11/5/25 Good Shepherd Sunday

My heart waits

With longing yet despair

My weakness controls my living.

I do not have the energy to climb the mountain

There to meet with the Lord.

Yet He loves the weak, the fallen

So He descends to my heart

'Come, rest and be still.

I do not ask of you what you cannot do

But you can Love

And that gives Me strength.

Let all you have to do

All you have to struggle with

Be offered with Love

And there You will meet Me

For that is the top of the mountain.

The path is that of Love.'

22/12/19

I long to see my beautiful Mother

She who trains my soul

Into the paths of fidelity

And loving obedience.

She is so loving and gentle

And comforts me when I fall

Like a little child who cries for Mama.

She must have been wonderful with the little Jesus.

And Joseph too, protective to both.

So many little children unloved and abused

Who need the love of the Holy Family

In our unhappy world.

Jesus, Mary and Joseph pray for us.

26/4/25

She came, staggering along, such tiny feet.
She gazed at You and smiled.
She stretched out her arms
And looked up at You, expecting tenderness.
You reached down and gently picked her up
And sat her on Your lap.
She felt Your Love
Snuggled into Your arms,
Quiet and peaceful.

Lord, may we be as trustful and simple
As we approach You
With our hearts open in faith.

Jesus Loved children. ' Let the children come to me, and do not hinder them; for to such belongs the kingdom of God.'
Luke 18:16

1/10/18

How radiant is the jewel

That is our Mother

Her Beauty transcends all spirits

Her Love like diamonds of grace

Purest of pure

None can be higher

In the firmament of saints

And yet her tender touch

Caresses all our pain

And cradles our hearts.

Amen

27/4/2022

I sense within my soul there is a deep space
Of encounter with something intangible.
Very peaceful, a sort of waiting for me
To come and rest. Friendly and kind,
Not intrusive.
Is this the place where we 'Live and move
And have our being?'
That mystery that indwells each soul.
The eternal Presence which encloses
All that there is- and ever shall be?

21/6/25

The Word passed by

Riding on the stars

His Creation to behold.

How it shone!

Enveloped in the glory of God

How it loved, how it lived

Unity and peace in every atom.

Even the angels joined in His merriment,

Flying from one star to another.

The saints sang, their voices pure harmony,

And Our Father chuckled, how He laughed,

His Spirit full of joy,

The Three together in Love,

Through all and for all.

30/5/18

The Three are the Father, Son and Holy Spirit.
The Trinity- God- in Christian faith.

The Grotto, Lourdes.

Like a murmuration
The prayers rose higher and higher
To our loving Mother's heart,
Circling and circling
Upwards to Heaven
To Our Father and Jesus ,His Son
For healing and blessing
Guidance and courage,
Myriads of souls in their beseeching,
The Love enfolding all.

17/9/24

There is a time for letting go

Not easy when Love calls the soul home

And those left behind hurt

To say 'goodbye.'

Yet the One who carries all mankind

Lifts the pain with memories of love and joy

Of delightful days and laughter

And the sweetness of loving where

All true goodness abounds.

We are not bereft but asked to wait

In patience and faith for that day

When we are reunited in the Love

That heals all grief and loss

And the sweetness of loving

Comes again

And for eternity.

4/6/2025

The Suffering of Jesus

Father, they know not
What they do
They do not know how to Love.
We have Loved them
From the beginning of the world.
They were seduced, taken by distortion
Of the good into the wrong path.
'I' not Thou, separated from the beauty
Of union where will is Trinitarian,
Seeks the good and fulfils,
Never divides.

So they fight, they hurt, they dominate,
They destroy to secure their will,
To control another,
Land, possessions, minds
And all is pain, suffering, cruelty.
The spirit is torn and bleeds.
So I brought them the way back to peace.
I offered them Myself
As the bridge of reunion.

24/6/25

I stared into Your Face
Your eyes in such pain
And yet Beauty shone through the pain
And filled my soul with peace
And Love.

 I am awestruck, here is my Saviour
Looking at me, His face bloody and sweaty,
His body contorted on this instrument of torture
And He thinks not about Himself
Only me.

This IS for you, He said: freedom of spirit.
I am speechless. Me? Yes, you, He said,
Especially you because I have rescued you from
Great danger.
I know. It is true. But ,surely,
Not just me- bringing back millions of souls
To the garden of Life where we find You,
Our Loving Saviour welcoming each one
To pastures new and beautiful.
Amen and Amen.

18/4/25

This Love is silent
Unheard but peaceful
A waiting Love
Undemanding
Yet I sense a longing
For a return
And a faint ache
A wondering if I will love
And comfort His pain
For He hangs in this silence
Bereft.

1/1/23

The Mother who looks down

From highest heaven

Looks with love and gentleness.

She sees each of us on our journey,

Understands our joys and sorrows

Blesses our longings for peace

Amid our troubled world.

She walked a difficult path,

Saw her Son rejected, falsely accused,

Suffered with Him in His dying

On the Cross.

Then in death held Him in her arms

This child of hers now Man

Who became her Saviour and Lord.

She became our Mother

And loves us , encourages and comforts,

If we will let her, for like her Son

She never intrudes,

Our Lady of loving help. So wonderful.

'He shall endure like the sun and the moon'
And the beauty of eternity will cover creation
No man shall be left alone, nor woman or child
For all will be wrapped in Love's embrace
And peace fill their souls when they turn
Their heart to God's whisper
Calling so gently 'Come to Me and rest'.

Psalm 71 verse 5

10/7/25

The Sacred Heart of Jesus is a wonderful place
Its mysteries abound and fear is no more
It is a spiritual country where my soul can walk
And drink of the healing streams of Love,
Attentive to all questions
And gently guiding and strengthening
Into peace and fulfilment.
The hurts of life are made better
Soothed and quietened
And I am rested.

Truly, God is my salvation
And I am so grateful.

11/7/25

Deep down into the depths

Flowed Love

Reaching each sin and enfolding it in Mercy

Every atom of Creation

Is washed in His Love,

Purified and made whole.

Yet few respond

And take His healing gift

So He hangs still

In agony

Lonely and unloved

Until all is fulfilled

And made one

In Joy.

31/3/25

You come into the darkness,

Light- to soothe and to heal,

Carry the pain into God

Where Love untangles and transforms

Into peace.

You are with each soul

Though they may not know.

You bear their journey

As a friend and Saviour

In silence,

Just outside the door of their soul,

Awaiting Invitation,

Never intruding.

The mystery of Love.

16/12/21

Two 'fun' poems

Our Loving Lord cares for us in old age and
some poetic licence about this donkey and
Our shepherd.

I am an old sheep now,

Bit unsteady on my legs

Yet my Master gently strokes my head

And He loves me.

He leads me to the pasture

Where He gives me food and water

And where I lie down and rest.

He knows what I need.

He cares for me with patience

And with Him I am safe.

5/6/25

I am a donkey
I plod along
I follow my Master
He is good to me.
He leads me to a stream,
There I drink.
I get thirsty carrying my load.

When I am very tired
I hang my head.
Then He takes the load off my back,
Makes me lie down and rest.
He waits by me, strokes my head,
Loving me.
Sometimes He will carry it Himself
Until I am strong enough to bear it again.

He is always gentle,
He knows when I need encouragement.
Then He gives me a big, juicy carrot.
I love my Master. He is so good to me.

If I make a wrong turn

He gently guides me back to the right path.

He is so patient.

I love my Master. He is so good to me

CONCLUSION

Now it is time to say 'farewell.' I hope that you have found something to cheer you, bless you, give you hope and encouragement.

May the Light within my soul reach out
And pervade the darkness
With the Love that fills the Light
And so transform all that is not of God.
May I stand firm on this Bridge of Love
Between the darkness and the Light
And pass the darkness I receive
Into the arms of God
Who will transform it into the energy of
Light and Union.

This is the work of the soul.

This is a Post Script for those who may want to know a little more about Jesus. It is just a simple attempt on my part.

The birth of Jesus and His ministry to His countrymen and women is a real story of the Love of God for His people. We read this story in the Gospels. The healing of the sick, the teaching about God, His Father and the way to find peace of soul through belief in Jesus- for In Jesus, God had become man.

Jesus was a threat to the religious leaders. He was the long awaited Messiah but not the triumphal figure Jewish tradition expected. He was gentle, humble and full of compassionate Love and people were drawn to him. The religious leaders were jealous and wanted to get rid of him. The story of how they did this and involved the Roman authorities is a story of treachery and lies but one which caused Jesus to be crucified.

This method of death was cruel and, in His innocence- for He had done nothing wrong- meant physical, mental, emotional and spiritual suffering.

His mission was to reunite mankind in spirit with God, to save His own people but also all mankind.

This is why.

In the beginning of creation God created man and woman. They chose not to walk in friendship with God and 'do their own thing 'instead. This ruptured the spiritual union with God and caused sin to pervade the soul of human nature. This is why we can be self centred, nasty, do what we want to do and 'hang everyone else'. And worse- mankind fights wars, kills people, is cruel, abusive.

Jesus had to heal this spiritual rupture in mankind. That was His mission. In His crucifixion, in the depths of His spirit, He took upon Himself, in

Love, the pain of this separation from God, the sinfulness that pervades our human nature. He became the sacrifice for all mankind in mind, body and spirit. He offered Himself in Love to His heavenly Father for the healing and restoration of this spiritual union. Through Him, our bridge to God, He paid the price for mankind's rebellion. He ransomed mankind through His Love, transformed rebellion into union so that in and through Him we are individually forgiven our sins. Yet we have to ask Him for this forgiveness. Through Him we can have peace, we can be held in His transforming Love as we journey in life.

After His death and burial and His work in the realm of the dead He was restored to Life. He appeared to many and instructed His disciples to tell the world of this good news, freely available to anyone who asks.

His Love for us is never ending.

In Him we become a new humanity, individually becoming transformed into this life of Love, helping and caring for others, sharing this Love. BUT transforming includes overcoming our faults and weaknesses! All we have to do is to ask Him for forgiveness. He knows life can be difficult. He said, "Come to me, all you who are weary and burdened, And I will give you rest." Because He also said

"I am the Way, the Truth and the Life."

Matthew 11:28

John 14:6

The proceeds of this book will go to the Order of Carmelites Discalced with my love and thanksgiving.

They need to renovate the Priory!